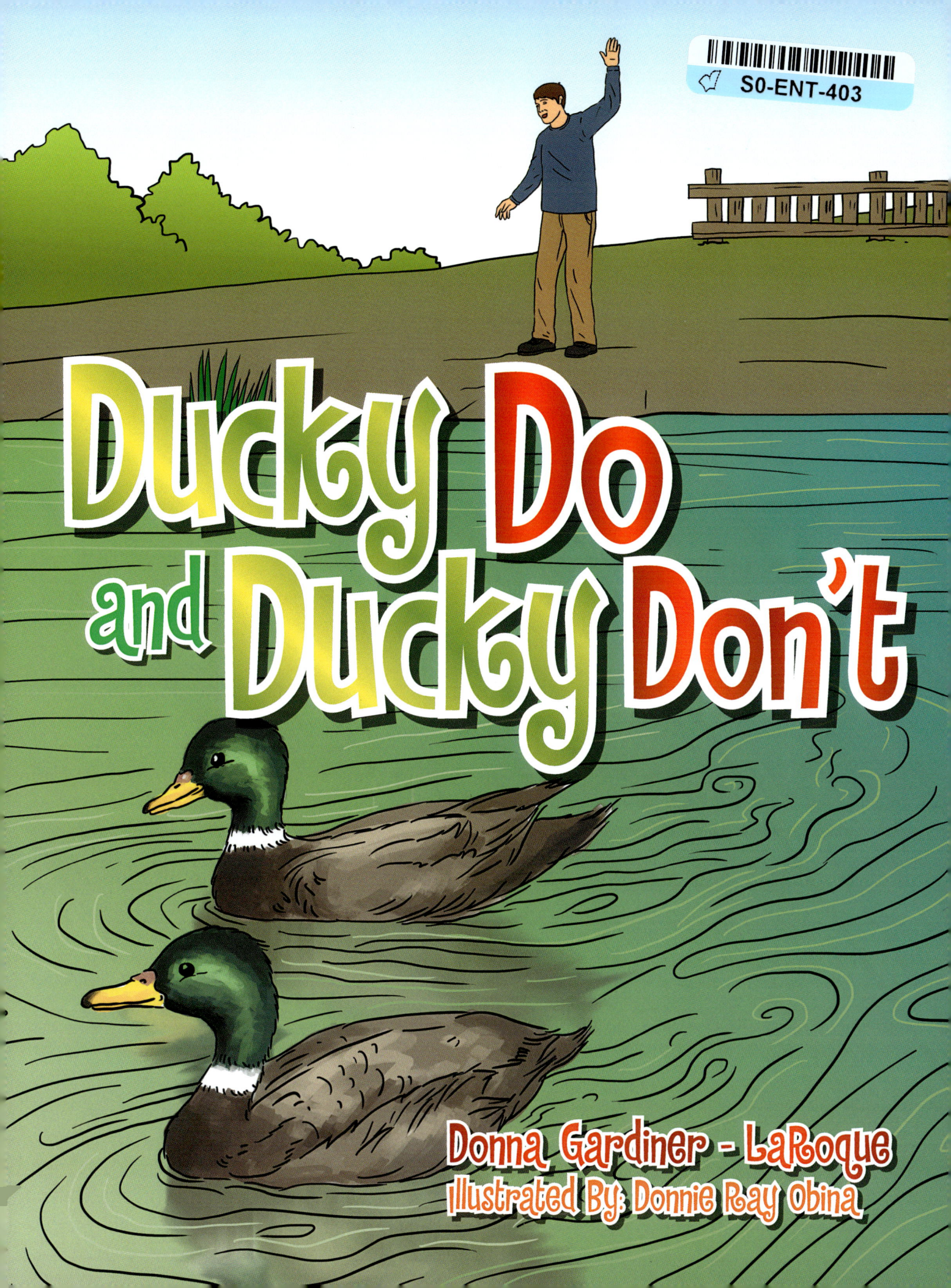

To Cohen, First Happy Birthday! Love, Aunt Evelyn

June 14, 2014

Copyright © 2013 by Donna Gardiner - LaRoque. 142501-LARO

ISBN: Softcover 978-1-4931-5318-3
EBook 978-1-4931-5319-0

All rights reserved. No part of this book may be reproduced or transmitted in any form or by any means, electronic or mechanical, including photocopying, recording, or by any information storage and retrieval system, without permission in writing from the copyright owner.

Rev. date: 12/15/2013

To order additional copies of this book, contact:
Xlibris LLC
1-888-795-4274
www.Xlibris.com
Orders@Xlibris.com

DEDICATION

I dedicate this book to my mother Evelyn Thompson that passed December 13, 2006. Also to my husband, James C. Gardiner, that passed July 11, 2010. And to my present husband, Thomas J. LaRoque, that gave me all the love and support in the process of publishing this book.

Ducky Do and Ducky Don't, say I will or say I won't, fly the creek or swim and float, Ducky Do and Ducky Don't.

One beautiful sunny day there were two little eggs on the riverbanks of Cobb Island. And momma duck and papa duck were nowhere to be found.

To make matters worse it was duck hunting season and all of the animals of the island knew this and feared the worst as they looked upon the two lonely little eggs.

All of a sudden the little animals were startled by a terrible noise in the bushes. Footsteps human footsteps! And they all scurried away.

And yes it was one of the hunters but there was a kindness in his face and sadness in his eyes as he looked upon the two lonely little eggs.

Feeling responsible he knew he could not leave them there, so he gently put one in each coat pocket, got in his boat and headed home.

When the kind hunter returned he reached into his pockets to get the little eggs and he was shocked to see there was a tiny hole in one of them. He thought he had accidentally broken it, but then he realized it was just hatching.

Reaching in his other coat pocket he was very excited to see that this egg also was showing signs of life. So he bundled the eggs up in a nice warm blanket, put them in a box and waited.

Soon it was morning but not just any morning. The kind hunter awakened to sounds of pitter patters and quack quacks in the box by his bed.

When he looked into the box two sweet little faces were looking up at him. It was at that moment he realized he had a big job ahead. He had to be both mama and papa to the tiny little mallards.

Gently he picked them up, so soft and so small and very hungry. Not sure of what to feed them, he called his neighbor farmer Chris and he rushed right over with a delicious bag of cracked corn.

After they ate they looked up at the kind hunter so sweetly. And he thought to himself how could he ever part with them but he knew the day would come when they would have to be released back into the wild.

Weeks passed and the two little mallard ducks were growing fast, their soft downy bodies were being replaced with beautiful feathers.

One day the kind hunter came home a little early only to find the naughty little ducks were making a terrible mess. He shouted ducky don't do! Ducky don't! It was at that moment he realized that would be the perfect names for them.

Ducky Do and Ducky Don't loved being with the kind hunter, everywhere he went they were with him. On any given day you could see the two little mallards following him as he did his daily tasks.

Fall turned to winter and winter turned to spring and the two little ducks were not so little anymore. They were fully grown proud and beautiful and ready to face the world.

The kind hunter knew this as he watched them looking out at the water. The river was calling out to them and Ducky Do and Ducky Don't could feel a longing for their wings to touch the sky.

The kind hunter loved them very much but he knew it was time to say goodbye to his friends. So he opened the gate and they all walked to the river's edge.

Ducky Do and Ducky Don't looked back at the kind hunter but they knew just as he did that they belonged in the wild and they were grateful for the good care he gave them.

As they swam away the kind hunter whispered to himself. My Ducky Do. My Ducky Don't, I do not will, nor do I want, to let you go, it breaks my heart ... Goodbye my Ducky Do my Ducky Don't.

The End

Edwards Brothers Malloy
Thorofare, NJ USA
April 4, 2014